ISBN 978-1-330-25783-8
PIBN 10003874

# 1 MONTH OF
# FREE
# READING

## at

## www.ForgottenBooks.com

By purchasing this book you are eligible for one month membership to ForgottenBooks.com, giving you unlimited access to our entire collection of over 700,000 titles via our web site and mobile apps.

To claim your free month visit:

www.forgottenbooks.com/free3874

# Similar Books Are Available from
# www.forgottenbooks.com

# Proceedings of the Society for Psychical Research.

## PART XLV.  Price 4/- net.

I. SOME EXPERIENCES IN HYPNOTISM, by "EDWARD GREENWOOD" (pseudonym).

II. MALAY SPIRITUALISM, by W. W. SKEAT, reprinted from Folk-Lore.

III. THE POLTERGEIST, HISTORICALLY CONSIDERED, by ANDREW LANG, with discussion by Frank Podmore.

IV. A DISCUSSION OF PROF. HYSLOP'S REPORT ON MRS. PIPER.
(a) Criticism by Hereward Carrington.
(b) Reply to above by Prof. Hyslop.
(c) Criticism by Frank Podmore.

**REVIEWS OF VARIOUS BOOKS.**

*READY.*

## PART XLVI.
### To be Issued in April or May.

PRESIDENTIAL ADDRESS, by SIR OLIVER LODGE.

REVIEWS OF MYERS' HUMAN PERSONALITY, by WILLIAM JAMES, SIR O. LODGE, PROF. FLOURNOY, of Geneva, etc.

R. BRIMLEY JOHNSON, Adelphi, LONDON.

# The Society for Psychical Research

## ITS RISE AND PROGRESS &
## A SKETCH OF ITS WORK

# THE SOCIETY FOR PSYCHICAL RESEARCH ITS RISE & PROGRESS & A SKETCH OF ITS WORK

### WITH FACSIMILE ILLUSTRATIONS OF THREE PAIRS OF THE THOUGHT-TRANSFERENCE DRAWINGS

BY

## EDWARD T. BENNETT

Assistant - Secretary to the Society, 1882-1902

"What a man affirms from his own experience is always worth listening to. What a man denies is rarely worth attention."
—Prof. W. F. BARRETT, F.R.S.

LONDON 1903
R. BRIMLEY JOHNSON
ADELPHI W.C.

# CONTENTS

# NOTE.

The writer is indebted to the Council of the Society for Psychical Research for kindly permitting quotations from the publications of the Society, and also for allowing the reproduction of some of the Thought-Transference Drawings.

# The Society for Psychical Research.

## CHAPTER I.

### Its Rise and Progress.

THE Society for Psychical Research was established in 1882, a little over twenty years ago. In January of that year a Conference of persons interested in certain branches of enquiry, which, in their opinion, had not received adequate attention and investigation from the literary and scientific world, met in London.

Six years previously, in 1876, Professor W. F. Barrett (now F.R.S.), of Dublin, read a Paper before the Meeting of the British Association in Glasgow, in which he gave a record of a series of experiments he had made, that led him to the belief that under certain conditions a transference of thoughts and ideas from one mind to another could occur, independently of the recognized channels of sensation. He urged the formation of a committee of scientific men to investigate this subject, along with other psychical phenomena, such as the so-called spiritistic manifestations which had been attested by distinguished men like Sir William Crookes and Dr. Alfred Russel Wallace. Owing to various causes, Professor Barrett's proposal fell through. The Paper, with some omissions and verbal alterations, is published in the *Proceedings* of the Society for Psychical Research, Vol. i., pp. 238—244. Professor Barrett returned to the question in letters to the *Times* and *Spectator* during 1876 and 1877, which elicited additional evidence. The results of further experiments on thought-transference in the normal (*i.e.*, not hypnotic) state are recorded by Professor Barrett in the columns of *Nature* for July 7th, 1881. At the conclusion of this letter Professor Barrett says:—"At the suggestion of Mr. G. J. Romanes I have arranged for a small committee of experts to verify or disprove the conclusions at which I have arrived." That committee met, but the publication of the result of their labours lay outside the functions of every recognized scientific body.

As the existing scientific societies and journals were concerned only with the study of natural or normal, as distinguished from transcendental phenomena, the formation of a new Society became desirable. Furthermore, it was felt that such a Society would give encouragement to, and continuity in, the investigation, not only of Thought-Transference, but of all that large group of phenomena outside the boundaries of orthodox science. Impressed with these views, and with the far-reaching importance of such an enquiry, Professor Barrett, after discussing the matter with scientific and other friends, took steps to convene a meeting on the subject. There also existed a desire for more systematic and scientific enquiry among many Spiritualists. Mr. E. Dawson Rogers, who for a number of years had taken a leading part among Spiritualists, strongly supported the view that an endeavour should be made to start a Society which might attract some of the best minds who had hitherto held aloof from public association with such a work, and placed at Professor Barrett's disposal a central hall in London, wherein a conference might be held. Mr. C. C. Massey also gave Professor Barrett much valued help and encouragement.

Professor Barrett undertook the invitation of a number of persons, some well known in science and literature, and others who had had long experience in occult phenomena, all of whom were animated with an earnest desire for a more systematic enquiry into these debatable regions hitherto unexplored by science. The result was that the Conference mentioned above, in the opening paragraph, was held. Professor Barrett presided, and gave a full statement as to the proposed scope of such a Society, and of the grounds which in his opinion rendered it absolutely necessary. A resolution, supported by the Rev. W. Stainton Moses, Mr. C. C. Massey, Mr. F. W. H. Myers, Mr. G. J. Romanes, and others, was unanimously passed in favour of such a course.

A Committee was appointed, which held several meetings, and presented a report to an adjourned Conference on February 20th, 1882, when the Society was definitely constituted. The earliest public announcement of the Society was made in the columns of "Light," a weekly journal, on the 25th of February, 1882. A list of sixteen names is given as constituting the first Council. It is remarkable as showing the changes which can take place in only twenty years, that of this list only two, Professor Barrett and the present writer, are left, who have continuously taken an active part in the work of the Society. Most of the other fourteen have been removed by death.

It was of inestimable value to the Society that Professor Henry Sidgwick, of Cambridge, consented to become its first President. He took an active part in drawing up the "Objects of the Society," the first official document which was issued. This document so well illustrates the courage on one hand, and the caution on the other, which was displayed in putting before the public the intentions of the founders of the Society, that a few extracts from it will not be out of place.

"It has been widely felt that the present is an opportune time for making an organised and systematic attempt to investigate that large group of debatable phenomena designated by such terms as mesmeric, psychical, and Spiritualistic.

"From the recorded testimony of many competent witnesses, past and present, including observations recently made by scientific men of eminence in various countries, there appears to be, amidst much illusion and deception, an important body of remarkable phenomena, which are *primâ facie* inexplicable on any generally recognised hypothesis, and which, if incontestably established, would be of the highest possible value.

"The task of examining such residual phenomena has often been undertaken by individual effort, but never hitherto by a scientific Society organised on a sufficiently broad basis."*

The following "Note," which is due mainly if not entirely to Professor Sidgwick, admirably states the position taken by the Society :—

"NOTE.—To prevent misconception, it is here expressly stated that Membership of this Society does not imply the acceptance of any particular explanation of the phenomena investigated, nor any belief as to the operation, in the physical world, of forces other than those recognised by Physical Science." †

This "Note" has been retained to the present time, in all editions of the "Objects of the Society."

The attitude of the public mind towards Psychical Research has so changed during the twenty years that it is difficult now

Proceedings, S.P.R., vol. i. p. 3

† Proceedings, S.P.R., vol. i. p. 5

to realize the feelings of contempt, which were almost universal among educated people, in regard to some branches of the enquiry; and it is also difficult to appreciate the amount of courage required on the part of persons occupying the positions of some of the founders of the Society, in thus embarking seriously on an investigation of this nature.

The first general meeting of the Society was held on July 17th, 1882, the President in the chair. A few paragraphs from his opening address will show the view which he entertained of the work in prospect.

" Before we proceed to what has been marked out as the business of this meeting, as it is the first general meeting of our new Society since the time it was definitely constituted, it has been thought that I should make a few brief remarks on the aims and methods of the Society, which will form a kind of explanation in supplement to our prospectus defining those aims and methods ;—which, I suppose, has been seen by all the members, and perhaps by some who are not as yet members. This prospectus has not been subjected to much instructive public criticism. I has been received, either with entire cordiality, or with guarded neutrality, or with uninstructive contempt.

" The first question I have heard is, Why form a Society for Psychica Research at all at this time, including in its scope not merely the phenomena of thought-reading (to which your attention will be directed chiefly this afternoon), but also those of clairvoyance and mesmerism, and the mass of obscure phenomena known as Spiritualistic? Well, in answering this, the first question, I shall be able to say something on which I hope we shall all agree ; meaning by "we," not merely we who are in this room, but we and the scientific world outside : and as, unfortunately, I have but few observations to make on which so much agreement can be hoped for, it may be as well to bring this into prominence, namely, that we are all agreed that the present state of things is a scandal to the enlightened age in which we live. That the dispute as to the reality of these marvellous phenomena,—of which it is quite impossible to exaggerate the scientific importance, if only a tenth part of what has been alleged by generally credible witnesses could be shewn to be true,—I say it is a scandal that the dispute as to the reality of these phenomena should still be going on, that so many competent witnesses should have declared their belief in them, that so many others should be profoundly interested in having the question determined, and yet that the educated world, as a body, should still be simply in the attitude of incredulity.

" Now the primary aim of our Society, the thing which we all unite to promote, whether as believers or non-believers, is to make a sustained and systematic attempt to remove this scandal in one way or another." *

* Proceedings, S.P.R., vol. i. pp. 7, 8.

Space will not permit of quotations from the President's replies to other questions. At the close of his address he says :

"Scientific incredulity has been so long in growing, and has so many and so strong roots, that we shall only kill it, if we are able to kill it at all as regards any of those questions, by burying it alive under a heap of facts. . We must accumulate fact upon fact, and add experiment upon experiment, and, I should say, not wrangle too much with incredulous outsiders about the conclusiveness of any one, but trust to the mass of evidence for conviction. The highest degree of demonstrative force that we can obtain out of any single record of investigation is, of course, limited by the trustworthiness of the investigator. We have done all that we can when the critic has nothing left to allege except that the investigator is in the trick. But when he has nothing else left to allege he will allege that.

"We shall, I hope, make a point of bringing no evidence before the public until we have got it to this pitch of cogency. . . . We must drive the objector into the position of being forced either to admit the phenomena as inexplicable, at least by him, or to accuse the investigators either of lying or cheating, or of a blindness or forgetfulness incompatible with any intellectual condition except absolute idiocy."*

The Society grew rapidly both in numbers, and in the Literary and Scientific position of its members. It has included many Fellows of the Royal Society, leading statesmen of opposite political parties, and many well-known names in all the Professions. The List of Members published in 1901 contains 948 names, while a separate Branch, comprising over 500 members, has existed in the United States since 1889. In 1883, as soon as the work began to increase, Mr. Edmund Gurney was appointed Hon. Secretary, which position he held until his death in 1888. Mr. F. W. H. Myers, and Mr. F. Podmore were then appointed joint Hon. Secretaries. In 1897 Mr. Myers alone was re-elected, Mr. Podmore remaining, however, a member of the Council. In 1899, Mr. J. G. Piddington was elected as co-Honorary Secretary, and since the election of Mr. Myers as President in 1900, he has held the position of Hon. Secretary by himself.

The successive Presidents of the Society have been :—

| | |
|---|---|
| Professor H. Sidgwick | 1882-1884. |
| Professor Balfour Stewart, F.R.S. ... | 1885-1887. |
| Professor H. Sidgwick ... ... | 1888-1892. |
| Right Hon. A. J. Balfour, M.P., F.R.S. | 1893. |
| Prof. William James (Harvard, U.S.A.) | 1894-1895. |
| Sir William Crookes, F.R.S. ... | 1896-1899. |
| Frederic W. H. Myers | 1900. |
| Sir Oliver Lodge, F.R.S. | 1901-1903. |

* Proceedings, S.P.R., vol. i. p. 12

It was an interesting co-incidence that in 1898, Sir William Crookes was President both of the British Association and of the Society for Psychical Research.

The first part of the *Proceedings* was published in October, 1882. Part XLI. was issued in 1901, completing a series of sixteen Volumes. In 1884, a *Journal* was started, to circulate monthly, among those belonging to the Society. One hundred and seventy-four Numbers, completing nine Volumes, had been issued up to the close of 1900. In addition to these Periodicals, an important work was published in 1886, under the title of " Phantasms of the Living " (two thick 8vo. vols.) under the joint authorship of Edmund Gurney, F. W. H. Myers, and F. Podmore, summarising the work of the Society up to that time in one comparatively small field. These works contain the formidable number of over 13,200 pages. It does not come within the purpose of this chapter to speak of the value of the work. But it may safely be said that no such amount of matter has ever been compiled, with such unremitting care as to the quality of the evidence brought forward, or with such caution as to the conclusions drawn from it. The total number of contributors is great. But by far the largest has been Mr. F. W. H. Myers, who, besides his share in " Phantasms of the Living," has written several series of articles in the *Proceedings*, as well as an immense number of communications of various kinds in both *Proceedings* and *Journal*. Part XLII. of the *Proceedings*, which commences the current Volume, consists of testimonies to his memory from Sir Oliver Lodge, and several other members of the Society. '

As might have been anticipated, the work of the Society did not develop exactly on the lines anticipated at the commencement. It may be classified under the five following departments. But between these there are no sharp dividing lines; they overlap and interlace in a curious and often unexpected manner :—

(1) The transmission of definite thoughts from one mind to another, by means independent of the ordinary organs of sense :—Thought-Transference or Telepathy.
(2) The nature, power, and effects of Suggestion:—Mesmerism,—Hypnotism,—Psychic Healing.
(3) Undeveloped and unrecognized Faculties of the Mind :—The Subliminal Self. ,
(4) Apparitions and Hauntings.

(5) Evidence of the existence of Intelligences other than "the Living," and of the reality of intercommunication.

This chapter may fitly conclude with some sentences from Mr. F. W. H. Myers' address, at the 105th General Meeting of the Society in May, 1900, after his election as President. He did not live to complete his year of office. It should be noted that he expressly says :—

"Throughout this address, of course, I am speaking for myself alone. I am not giving utterance to any collective view."*

"We [Psychical Researchers] have enough and to spare of such motives as appeal to ordinary men. We have the stimulus of intellectual curiosity,—more richly satisfied, I think, in ours than in any other quest ;—and beyond this, most of us, I think, have the healthful, primary desire for the prolongation — the endless prolongation — of life and happiness. . . Usually, when a man cares little for existence, this is because existence cares little for him. . . It has been doubt as to the value of life and love which has made the decadence of almost all civilizations. Life is the final aim of life ; the mission of the highest Teacher was that we might have it the more abundantly; and the universe strives best towards its ultimate purpose through the normal, vigorous spirit to whom to live itself is joy." †

---

* Proceedings, S.P.R., vol. xv. p. 119.
† Proceedings, S.P.R., vol. xv. p. 113.

# CHAPTER II.

## THOUGHT-TRANSFERENCE OR TELEPATHY.

IN the previous chapter the work of the Society was classified under five departments, the first being—" The transmission of definite thoughts from one mind to another, by means independent of the ordinary organs of sense." This chapter will be devoted to the evidence in support of Thought-Transference as a hitherto unrecognized fact in Science. The evidence in favour of a fact may be divided into two classes : (1) experiments made for the purpose of testing the alleged fact, and (2) testimony to occurrences spontaneously arising, seemingly incapable of explanation on any ordinary hypothesis. We will take the case of experiments first.

The earliest systematic work of the Society was the institution of series of experiments, of a variety of kinds, to ascertain whether such transference of definite thoughts was a reality. The first requisite in the experiments was to exclude the agency of the five senses, seeing, hearing, tasting, smelling, and feeling. Four of these presented no difficulty. But with regard to the sense of touch, it was soon found that " unconscious muscular action" was a subtle factor, the extent of which it was extremely difficult to determine, and that as a conceivable explanation it threw doubt on all cases of transmission of thought where there was the slightest possibility of its agency. The extent to which " unconscious muscular action" has been called upon to explain apparent thought-transference, seems at times to approach the limits of absurdity, as, for instance, when the transmitter and receiver are connected merely by a slack piece of string. But, to be on the safe side, the Society soon wisely decided to exclude all experiments in which there was contact of any kind between transmitter and receiver.

At the first General Meeting of the Society, held on July 17th, 1882, Professor W. F. Barrett read the " First Report on Thought-Reading " written by himself, Mr. Gurney, and Mr. Myers. The object of the Report was to place on record the first instalment of the evidence as to whether "a vivid impression or a distinct idea in one mind can be communicated to another mind without the intervening help of the recognised organs of sensation."* The wonderful change which has taken place since that time, in the attitude of the public mind, and which has already been referred to, is aptly illustrated by a remark which the writers of this Report make on its first page. They say:—"The present state of scientific opinion throughout the world is not only hostile to any belief in the possibility of transmitting a single mental concept, except through the ordinary channels of sensation, but, generally speaking, it is hostile even to any enquiry upon the matter. Every leading physiologist and psychologist down to the present time has relegated what, for want of a better term, has been called "Thought-reading" to the limbo of exploded fallacies."†

Several series of experiments are described in detail in the Reports of the Committee. Space will only permit of a reference to one of these, selected because all who took part in it were members of the Society deeply interested in the work.‡ Mr. Edmund Gurney and Mr. F. W. H. Myers conducted the experiments. Mr. Douglas Blackburn and Mr. G. A. Smith were "transmitter" and "receiver." In some of these earliest experiments, Mr. B. and Mr. S. held hands. In some there was no contact. A colour or a name was written down and shown to Mr. B., and Mr. S. then attempted to give it. Or, a particular spot, say, on the arm of Mr. B., was rendered painful, and Mr. S. endeavoured to localise it. All ordinary means of knowledge were, of course, carefully excluded. Under these circumstances, in a series of twenty-three experiments, about half the answers may be considered absolutely correct several of the others nearly so, and none were entirely wide of the mark. The hypothesis of coincidence is practically excluded, in view of the number of similar results obtained.

A second Report by the same writers was read at a Meeting of the Society held in December, 1882. In addition to further experiments of the same nature as those described in the first Report, some of an entirely different kind were made, and with a different set of persons. These consist of " Thought-Transference Drawings," done thus:—A. makes an outline sketch of a simple geometrical figure, or of something a little more elaborate. B.

* Proceedings, S.P.R., vol. i, p. 13.

† Proceedings, S.P.R., vol. i. p. 13.

‡ Proceedings, S.P.R., vol. i. pp. 78-80.

sees this sketch, and carrying it in his mind, goes and stands behind C., who sits with a pencil and paper before him and draws the impression he receives from B.  All ordinary precautions are taken, and, except in a few trials, no contact between any of the parties was permitted.  A series of experiments of this nature is given in the Second Report, and a further series, under very stringent conditions, is given in a Third Report read at a Meeting in April, 1883.

Similar series of experiments have been carried out by several sets of " transmitters " and " receivers," and with similar results.

Plates I., II., and III. are facsimiles of three of these pairs of " Thought-Transference " drawings.*

We will now turn to the second class of evidence for Thought-Transference :—The testimony as to occurrences spontaneously arising which seem incapable of explanation on any accepted hypothesis.  This is a very wide field, and we must be content with a small number of examples, of the accuracy and good faith of which there is no moral doubt.

CASE I.—The narrator is the wife of General R.—"On September 9th 1848, at the siege of Mooltan, Major-General R., C.B., then adjutant of his regiment, was most severely and dangerously wounded, and supposing himself dying, asked one of the officers with him to take the ring off his finger and send it to his wife, who, at the time, was fully 150 miles distant, at Ferozepore.   On the night of September 9th, 1848, I was lying on my bed, between sleeping and waking, when I distinctly saw my husband being carried off the field, seriously wounded, and heard his voice saying, " Take this ring off my finger and send it to my wife."   All the next day I could not get the sight or the voice out of my mind.   In due time I heard of General R. having been severely wounded in the assault at Mooltan. He survived, however, and is still living.   It was not for some time after the siege that I heard from Colonel L., the officer who helped to carry General R. off the field, that the request as to the ring was actually made to him, just as I heard it at Ferozepore at that very time.   M.A.R."†

CASE II.—Communicated by a medical man—Dr. C. Ede, of Guildford to whom the incident was related by both ladies.—"Lady G. and her sister had been spending the evening with their mother, who was in her usual health and spirits when they left her.   In the middle of the night the sister awoke in a fright, and said to her husband, ' I must go to my mother at once ; do order the carriage.   I am sure she is taken ill.'   The husband, after trying in vain to convince his wife that it was only a fancy, ordered the carriage.   As she was approaching her mother's house, where two

---

* Proceedings, S.P.R., vol. i. pp. 83, 89, and 93.

† Proceedings, S.P.R., vol. i. p. 30.

roads meet, she saw Lady G.'s carriage. When they met, each asked the other why she was there. The same reply was made by both. ' I could not sleep, feeling sure that mother was ill, and so I came to see.' As they came in sight of the house, they saw their mother's confidential maid at the door, who told them when they arrived that their mother had been taken suddenly ill and was dying, and had expressed an earnest wish to see her daughters." *

CASE III.—Reported by the Literary Committee, consisting of Prof. W. F. Barrett, Mr. Edmund Gurney, Mr. C. C. Massey, Rev. W. Stainton Moses, and Mr. F. W. H. Myers. " A mesmerist, well known to us, was requested by a lady to mesmerise her, in order to enable her to visit in spirit certain places of which he himself had no knowledge. He failed to produce this effect; but found that he could lead her to describe places unknown to her but familiar to him. Thus on one occasion he enabled her to describe a particular room which she had never entered, but which she described in perfect conformity with his recollection of it. It then occurred to him to imagine a large open umbrella as lying on a table in this room, whereupon the lady immediately exclaimed, " I see a large open umbrella on the table." †

CASE IV.—Communicated by Mr. R. Fryer, of Bath.—"A strange experience occurred in the Autumn of the year 1879. A brother of mine had been from home for 3 or 4 days, when one afternoon at half-past 5 (as nearly as possible), I was astonished to hear my name called out very distinctly. I so clearly recognised my brother's voice that I looked all over the house for him ; but not finding him, and indeed knowing he must be distant some 40 miles, I ended by attributing the incident to a fancied delusion, and thought no more about the matter. On my brother's arrival home, however, on the sixth day, he remarked amongst other things that he had narrowly escaped an ugly accident. It appeared that whilst getting out from a railway carriage he missed his footing, and fell along the platform ; by putting out his hands quickly he broke the fall, and only suffered a severe shaking. 'Curiously enough,' he said, 'when I found myself falling I called out your name.' This did not strike me for a moment, but on my asking him during what part of the day this happened, he gave me the time, which I found corresponded exactly with the moment I heard myself called."‡

CASE V.—Communicated by Dr. Joseph Smith, for many years leading medical practitioner in Warrington.—"When I lived at Penketh, about 40 years ago, I was sitting one evening, reading, and a voice came to me saying, 'Send a loaf to James Gandy's.' Still I continued reading, and the voice came to me again, 'Send a loaf to James Gandy's.' Still I continued reading, when a third time the voice came to me with great

* Proceedings, S.P.R., vol. i. p. 31.

† Proceedings, S.P.R., vol. i. p. 120.

‡ "Phantasms of the Living," vol. ii., p. 103.

emphasis, 'Send a loaf to James Gandy's'; and this time it was accompanied by an almost irresistible impulse to get up. I obeyed this impulse, and went into the village, bought a large loaf, and seeing a lad at the shop door, I asked him if he knew James Gandy's. He said he did ; so I gave him a trifle and asked him to take the loaf there, and to say a gentleman had sent it. Mrs. Gandy was a member of my class (in connection with the Wesleyan Methodist Church), and I went down the next morning to see what had come of it, when she told me that a strange thing had happened to her last night. She said she wanted to put the children to bed, and they began to cry for food, and she had not any to give them ; for her husband had been four or five days out of work. She then went to pray, to ask God to send them something, soon after which a lad came to the door with a loaf, which he said a gentleman gave him to bring to her. I calculated, upon enquiry made of her, that her prayer and the voice which I heard exactly coincided in point of time." *

CASE VI.—Abstract of a communication from the Rev. R. H. Killick, Great Smeaton Rectory, Northallerton.—A much loved little daughter was at home. I was in Paris. One Sunday afternoon all at once I seemed to hear a voice say, "Etta has fallen into the pond." I tried to banish the thought, but in vain. At night I went to bed, but not to sleep. (It was before the days of telegraphs). In course of time I had letters saying all were well. I finished my journey and never spoke of my "foolish nervousness." Some months afterwards I was at a dinner party, and the hostess said, "What did you say about Etta when you heard ?" "Heard what ?" I said. "Oh !" said the lady, "Have I let out a secret ?" I said, "I don't leave till I learn." She said, "Don't get me into trouble, but I mean about her falling into the pond." "What pond ?" "Your pond," "When ?" "While you were abroad," I hastened home, sought our governess and enquired what it all meant. She said, "Oh, how cruel to tell you now it's all over? Well, one Sunday afternoon we were walking by the pond and Theodore said, 'Etta, it's so funny to walk with your eyes shut.' So she tried, and fell into the water. I heard a scream, and looked round and saw Etta's head come up, and I ran and seized her and pulled her out. Oh it was so dreadful! And then I carried her up to her mamma, and she was put to bed, and soon got all right." I enquired the day. It was the very Sunday I was in Paris, and had this dreadful conviction. I asked the hour. About 4 o'clock! The very time, also, that the unwelcome thought plunged into my mind. I said, "Then it was revealed to me in Paris the instant it happened ;" and, for the first time, I told her of my sad experience in Paris on that Sunday afternoon. I had ten children at home at the time.†

It will be obvious to the reader that the brief summary of the results of Thought-Transference given above, and the six cases of spontaneous Thought-Transference quoted, convey a most in-

* "Phantasms of the Living," vol. ii., pp. 123-4.
† "Phantasms of the Living" vol. ii., pp. 119-120.

PLATE I.

ORIGINAL DRAWING.

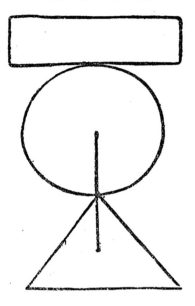

REPRODUCTION.

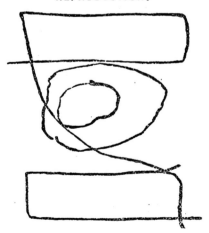

**PLATE II.**

ORIGINAL DRAWING.

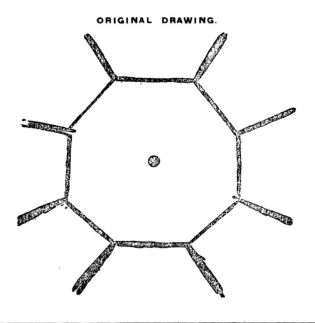

REPRODUCTION.

**PLATE III.**

ORIGINAL DRAWING.

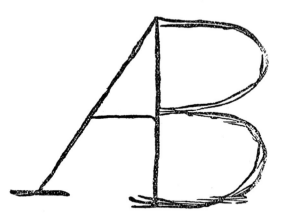

REPRODUCTION

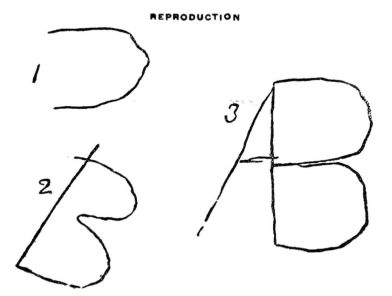

The Figures in this drawing indicate successive attempts, as if the mental picture were " glimpsed " piecemeal.

adequate idea of the amount of evidence collected by the Society. In " Phantasms of the Living " alone, there are whole chapters devoted to cases where definite ideas and matters of fact appear to be transmitted between persons at great distances from each other· The conclusion seems to be irresistible, that the five senses do not exhaust the means by which knowledge may enter the mind. In other words, the investigator seems to be driven to the conclusion that Thought-Transference or Telepathy must now be included among scientifically proved facts. The interpretation of the facts, the means by which knowledge is thus conveyed, the mode of its transmission, belong to a different branch of the enquiry.

Although the value of the evidence already collected cannot be reasonably disputed, nor the grand conclusion to which it points be denied, it is extremely important that the amount of evidence in support of Telepathy should be greatly increased. Experiments can be conducted in such a variety of ways, that it is possible for almost any careful or intelligent group of persons to carry out what may prove to be of real value to the cause of science. Care as to conditions and complete and correct noting down of results at the time, are the essentials for such experiments to be of value. The Society would greatly value reports of such careful investigation.

# CHAPTER III.

## SUGGESTION.—HYPNOTISM.—PSYCHIC HEALING.

IN this chapter it is proposed to give a brief review of what the Society has done towards explaining the nature, power, and effects of Suggestion, with special reference to Mesmerism, Hypnotism, and Psychic Healing.

## SUGGESTION.—HYPNOTISM.

The second and third volumes of the Proceedings of the Society contain several articles, from both the separate and the joint pens of Mr. Gurney and of Mr. Myers, dealing with the interpretation of the phenomena of Suggestion, Mesmerism, and Hypnotism. They are extremely interesting as early attempts to evolve order out of a wilderness of facts and a chaos of theories. But it must be confessed that to the ordinary reader the effect is bewildering. In an elaborate article by Mr. Myers, in Volume V., entitled "On Telepathic Hypnotism," light begins to dawn. The nucleus of the paper consists of observations on a remarkable hypnotic sensitive, made by Mr. Myers himself at Havre in 1886. The most striking feature of the case was the production of sleep and other hypnotic phenomena by the will or mental suggestion of a person at a distance from the subject. Incidentally Mr. Myers gives a definition of the distinction between "Mesmerism" and "Hypnotism" which it may be useful to quote, slightly simplifying the wording. He speaks of the elder English school of Mesmerists as "believers in a specific vital effluence or influence," as opposed to Hypnotists proper, whom he describes as "believers in a mechanical agency alone in the induction of trance." He points out that the Mesmerists have "altogether missed the distinction between the exercise of vital influence in the presence of [or in the] immediate proximity of the subject, and its exercise at a distance say of half a mile." He also points out that "more cautious observers have consciously dismissed the difficulty as insoluble. For convenience sake they use the analogy of *suggestion*, and speak of suggestion at

a distance," but make no attempt to connect this distant suggestion with suggestion in the actual presence of the subject.
Mr. Myers says :—

"In my own view also (1886) no complete solution of the problem is
possible. We are entirely ignorant of the nature of the force which may be
supposed to be operative in the production of telepathic phenomena,—to
impel or facilitate the passage of thoughts or sensations from one mind to
another without the intervention of the recognised organs of sense."*

Yet Mr. Myers thinks it possible to attempt something. He
says :—

"In order to get any clearness into our notions we must attack at once
the extremely difficult question, What do we mean by suggestion?
The word suggestion as a cause of the hypnotic trance may have at least
four different meanings, viz. : (1) verbal suggestion; (2) self suggestion ;
(3) mental suggestion from a person present; (4) mental suggestion from a
person absent."†

Mr. Myers proceeds to treat the subject at length, and, as to his
own convictions, says :—

"I hold that the enigma of hypnotism has no single answer which solves
it.  .  .  I hold emphatically that hypnotic changes are primarily physiological rather than pathological—supernormal rather than abnormal."‡

That is to say, in more familiar language, these phenomena do
not indicate a diseased condition which ought to be feared or
suppressed, but should be looked upon as gateways to a higher
knowledge, and therefore worthy of investigation and certain to
reward it. From this time the word "mesmerism" was almost if
not entirely dropped by the leading investigators of the Society.

As illustrating the character of the phenomena which Mr. Myers
witnessed at Havre, in the case which forms the nucleus of the
paper quoted from above, the following is selected. Adequate
precaution was taken against three possible sources of error :—
Fraud, accidental coincidence, and suggestion by word or gesture.
Madame B., a peasant woman, lives with a sister of Dr. Gibert's at
a house called the Pavillon, about two-thirds of a mile distant from
Dr. Gibert's own house and dispensary. Mr. Myers says :—

Proceedings, S.P.R., vol. iv. pp. 138-9.

† Proceedings, S.P.R., vol. iv. pp. 139-140.

‡ Proceedings, S.P.R., vol. iv. p. 141.

"On the morning of April 22nd we again selected by lot an hour (11 a.m.) at which M. Gibert should will, from his dispensary, that Madame B. should go to sleep in the Pavillon. . . At 11.25 we entered the Pavillon quietly, and almost at once she descended from her room to the *salon*, profoundly asleep. . . In the evening we all dined at M. Gibert's, and M. Gibert made another attempt to put her to sleep at a distance from his house in the Rue Séry— she being at the Pavillon, Rue de la Ferme—and to bring her to his house by an effort of will. At 8.55 he retired to his study ; and MM. Ochorowicz, Marillier, Janet, and A. T. Myers went to the Pavillon and waited outside in the street out of sight of the house. At 9.22 Dr. Myers observed Madame B. coming halfway out of the garden-gate and again retreating. Those who saw her more closely observed that she was plainly in the somnambulic state, and was wandering about and muttering, At 9.25 she came out (with eyes persistently closed, so far as could be seen), walked quickly past MM. Janet and Marillier without noticing them, and made for M. Gibert's house     . At 9.45 she reached the street in front of M. Gibert's house. There she met him, but did not notice him, and walked nto his house, where she rushed hurriedly from room to room on the ground floor. M. Gibert had to take her hand before she recognised him. She then grew calm."*

One of the most curious branches of Hypnotic enquiry is "post-hypnotic suggestion." To many who have never witnessed anything of the kind, the facts are simply incredible. The fourth volume of the "Proceedings" already quoted, contains an article by Mr. Gurney on "Peculiarities of Certain Post-Hypnotic States." The following instances must suffice. Mr. Gurney writes :—

"One of my recent 'subjects,' who was told that at a certain time after waking he was to poke the fire—which would, of course, be an odd thing for him to do unasked in my room—when the time arrived, turned to me and asked politely if I should object to his poking the fire. Another 'subject' was told during his trance that when I rose from my seat for the fourth time he was to blow out a particular candle close to which my wife was sitting at work. He was woke and conversed with me in a perfectly natural manner. I rose from my seat at intervals, took a few paces through the room or stood at the fire for a few seconds, and sat down again. On the fourth occurrence of this the lad got up, saying, 'There is too much light here,' but instead of at once fulfilling the order, he had sufficient forethought and courtesy to take another candle from another table and to place it where the one he was to blow out stood ; after which he blew out the right one. Questioned some minutes afterwards, he perfectly remembered what he had done."†

* Proceedings, S.P.R., vol. iv. pp. 133-4.

† Proceedings, S.P.R., vol. iv. p. 270.

In 1890 the Council of the Society issued a circular, which was extensively circulated, entitled, " Hypnotism: Its Conditions and Safeguards." It is included in Volume VII. of the " Proceedings." Its object is stated in the opening sentence, " So many sensational and exaggerated reports of the effects and dangers of hypnotism have recently appeared in the public Press, that a brief and sober statement of what, so far as our present knowledge extends, hypnotism can actually effect may perhaps be beneficial."* The circular says:—

" It should be borne in mind that the hypnotic state is not, in the ordinary sense of the word, morbid."* " Though the probable evils of hypnotism have been much exaggerated, there are serious dangers to be guarded against. It is indeed by no means a subject to be played with "† " No one should suffer himself to be hypnotised except for therapeutic or scientific purposes."§ " Where hypnotism is employed for curative purposes the treatment has proved often beneficial and always harmless."§ "And where it has been employed for experiment and demonstration only, the effects on the subject, in careful hands, have proved equally satisfactory. The young men and boys on whom the Society for Psychical Research has conducted numerous experiments . . have always been, and remain to this day, in full health, physically and morally." §

The twelfth volume of the " Proceedings " (1896-7) contains two important articles by Dr. J. Milne Bramwell, " Personally Observed Hypnotic Phenomena," and " What is Hypnotism ? " Dr. Charles Lloyd Tuckey's book on "Treatment by Hypnotism and Suggestion" has passed through four editions. The latest, issued in 1900, is a volume of several hundred pages, addressed primarily to the medical profession. Dr. Bramwell and Dr. Tuckey have both been members of the Council of the Society for many years.

## Psychic Healing.

The subject of Psychic Healing is a very wide one. "Suggestion," in one of its many forms, enters far more largely into all branches of the healing art, orthodox and unorthodox, than is generally recognised. The ordinary treatment of the physician abounds in it, and it even enters into surgical cases. Very curious instances may be cited on the authority of Sir Humphrey Davey,

---

* Proceedings, S.P.R., vol. vii., p. 137.

†Proceedings, S.P.R., vol. vii., p. 138

§Proceedings, S.P.R., vol. vii. p. 139.

Sir Benjamin Brodie, and other first-class names. But a com-mencement has hardly even yet been made of a systematic examina-tion of the whole subject. Facts and cases have not yet been adequately examined and classified. An attempt has been made to draw a line between nervous cases, or cases due more or less to the imagination, and actual physical or organic cases. It has been alleged that only the former class are amenable to psychic treat-ment. But experience does not justify this conclusion. Physical and organic effects, even diseases, can be caused simply by mental impression. It seems, therefore, unreasonable to reject the idea that mental treatment may be efficacious as a remedial agent, not only in nervous disorders and in what may be called imaginary ailments, but also in cases of organic disease, even in cases which under ordinary circumstances require surgical treatment. In the enquiry of the Society into Psychic Healing two great difficulties presented themselves. The first was to feel sure that there was really anything the matter with the patient, that the case was not simply one of nerves or fancy, and which would disappear if the patient could be roused from his mental state. Of course, even this might be called psychic healing; but it is not what is ordinarily meant by it. The second difficulty was of another kind. The Society took up the position, though it was not explicitly laid down as a rule, that it would not admit alleged cures as of evidential value, unless the condition of the patient was vouched for by the testimony of duly qualified medical men, both before and after This may have been wise. But it had the effect of greatly restrict-ing the amount of evidence at the disposal of the Society. With regard to the first difficulty the effect was that the results obtained were mostly negative. A member of the Society resided for some time at " Bethshan," an institution of a religious character, where it was alleged, remarkable cures had been effected. But no cases presented themselves in which it could be definitely asserted that special psychic treatment produced a cure. A visit was paid to Lourdes by Dr. A. T. Myers and Mr. F. W. H. Myers, and a report presented in the form of an extremely painstaking article under the title of " Mind-Cure, Faith-Cure, and the Miracles of Lourdes." As a " provisional judgment " on the " various groups of facts thus far recorded," the writers say:—

" No one of the special forms of pyscho-therapeutics which we were asked to examine has yet produced evidence definite enough to satisfy reasonable men of any miraculous agency, however surprising the cure may sound. Many forms of psycho-therapeutics produce, by obscure but natural agencies, for which at present we have no better terms than suggestion and self-suggestion, effects to which no definite limit can yet be assigned." *

With regard to the second difficulty, the etiquette of the medical profession, and in some cases, it must be said, the prejudices of its members, presented an effectual barrier against the conditions laid down being complied with. A striking case of this came under the notice of the writer. In the course of his work he investigated an alleged cure of life-long disease or malformation of the leg and foot. The facts were very simple. A child of persons in humble circumstances—a girl—had been treated from infancy until after her marriage, by surgical instrument makers, under the advice of hospital surgeons. She had always worn an iron instrument on one leg and foot, and had never in her life worn or bought a *pair* of boots or shoes. After a very few treatments by a well-known Australian healer, then in London, she was able to walk across the room without any artificial aid. Before long she bought a pair of boots to her great delight, and could walk a reasonable distance without any mechanical appliance. First-hand testimony was obtained from the young woman herself, from her mother who had carried her as a child to the hospital, and from her husband. The pathetic thankfulness of the mother was quite affecting. She could only say, almost in the words of the New Testament : " One thing I know, that whereas she was lame, she can now walk." After the cure had been effected, it was found impracticable to obtain any adequate statement as to the history of the case from the hospital and surgical authorities, or any official testimony as to the change in their patient. They were clearly in this dilemma—either a notable cure had been effected, or they had misjudged the nature of the case for over twenty years, and had burdened the patient with needless expenditure of time and money, and a vast amount of trouble and anxiety. The result was that the case was ignored by the Society.

One particular direction in which the power of Psychic Healing is no longer open to question, and also one which will appeal to the public mind as eminently practical, is in the cure of dipsomania. The results are numerous and remarkable. Space will not admit of more than two instances being cited, both given by Dr. Bramwell from his own notes, in an address at the Annual Meeting of the British Medical Association in 1898.

*Proceedings, S.P.R., vol. ix. p. 204.

"*Case 6.*—Dipsomania.—Mr. E., aged 33, April 30th, 1890.  He had a family history of intemperance, and commenced to take stimulants in excess at seventeen.  In 1884 his friends induced him to place himself under control.  This was repeated thrice without good results.  In 1887 he entered a retreat for a year, but soon after leaving it began to drink as badly as ever.  From this time  .  .  any physical pain or mental trouble would start a drinking bout, and of these he had on an average one a week.  He was hypnotised from April 30th to May 17th, 1890, and during this time kept sober.  He returned home and relapsed in less than a month.  He was again hypnotised daily for a week, and from that date, June, 1890, until the present time he has not relapsed,"*

"*Case 7.*—Dipsomania.—A patient, aged 47, with bad family history of alcoholism.  He had taken stimulants to excess for seventeen years, had had three attacks of delirium tremens and seven of epilepsy.  He was first hypnotised on April 22nd, 1895, and has not relapsed since."*

The substance of some remarks of Mr. Myers' in an address given (by special permission) to the British Medical Association in the same year as Dr. Bramwell's are appropriate and suggestive.  The following is partly quotation and partly summary :—

The essential meaning of Hypnotism is always the same—a fuller control over subliminal plasticity.  But, after all, how is this fuller control effected?  How is this subliminal plasticity—this *vis medicatrix Naturæ*—actually reached ?  The purely physiological explanation is absolutely insufficient.  The main consensus of living hypnotists declares that hypnotic phenomena are due to *suggestion*, almost or quite alone.  We need not reject their dictum, but we must make it our task to try and find out what that word suggestion can mean.  One thing the word certainly cannot mean, and that is —mere ordinary persuasiveness.  Dr. Bramwell is not the first person who has advised the dipsomaniac not to drink.  If he succeeds in reforming such a patient it is because he has managed to touch, not his supraliminal reason, but his subliminal plasticity.  He has set going some intelligent organic faculty in the man, which has lain dormant until that moment, and which proves more effectual for healing than the man's conscious will.  How has he done this ?  He has either infused power or he has merely evoked it.  He has either added power by some influence, or he has unlocked some fountain of energy which was latent within the man's own being.  Beneath the threshold of waking consciousness there lies, not merely an unconscious complex of organic processes, but an intelligent vital control. To incorporate that profound con_ trol with our waking will is the great evolutionary end which Hypnotism is beginning to help us to attain.*

Mr. Myers illustrates his position by the following analogy:—

" In waking consciousness I am like the proprietor of a factory whose machinery I do not understand. My foreman—my subliminal self—weaves for me so many yards of broadcloth per diem (my ordinary vital processes) as a matter of course. If I want any pattern more complex I have to shout my orders in the din of the factory, where only two or three inferior work- men hear me, and shift their looms in a small and scattered way. Such are the confused and capricious results of the first, the more familiar stages of hypnotic suggestion. At certain intervals, indeed, the foreman stops most of the looms, and uses the freed power to stoke the engine and to oil the machinery. This, in my metaphor, is sleep, and it will be effective hypnotic trance if I can get the foreman to stop still more of the looms, come out of his private room, and attend to my orders—my self-suggestions—for their repair and re-arrangement. The question for us proprietors then is, how we can best get at our potent but secluded foremen ; in what way we can make to our subliminal selves effective suggestions. And here I think we are for the present at the end of theory. We must look for guidance to actual experience, not to hypnotism alone, but to all forms of self-suggestion which are practically found to remove and soothe the pains and weariness of large masses of common men."†

After referring to " two popular forms of self-suggestion "— the healing fountain of Lourdes, and so-called Christian Science—as types of the rest, Mr. Myers concludes by saying :—

" Finally, if beneath the fanaticism and the extravagance of men blindly seeking relief from pain, some glimmering truth makes way, that truth also it must be for science to adopt and to utilize, to clarify and to interpret. By one method or other—and her familiar method of widespread cautious experiment should surely be the best—science must subject to her own deliberate purposes that intelligent vital control, that reserve of energy which lies beneath the conscious threshold, and works obscurely for the evolution of man."‡

---

*Proceedings, S.P.R., vol. xiv. pp. 106-7.
†Proceedings, S.P.R., vol. xiv. pp. 107-8.
‡Proceedings, S.P.R., vol. xiv. p. 108.

# CHAPTER IV.

## THE SUBLIMINAL SELF.

IT was unquestionably a wise course, adopted by the Society in its early days, to devote most of its attention and energy in the first place to those branches of Psychical Enquiry which were, so to speak, just outside the pale of orthodox science and literature. The amount and intensity of opposition to the work of the Society was thus materially mitigated; and the gulf which, in the minds of most people, separates physical from psychical investigation was narrowed if not bridged over. Thought-reading and Telepathy, Mesmerism and Hypnotism thus came in for the greatest share of attention. It is true that among the earliest committees appointed was one on "Haunted Houses." But the main work of the Society was in the direction indicated by Telepathy and Hypnotism. The grand fact of Telepathy was conclusively proved. The reality of the varied phenomena of Hypnotism was indisputable. The evidence presented in chapters II. and III. justifies these assertions. It rapidly became evident that beyond Telepathy and Hypnotism there existed an almost unknown land, a wilderness of facts and phenomena, unsystematized, many of them apparently isolated, and wholly ignored by, and unconnected with, any recognized branch of science and philosophy. To the exploration and study of this new world Mr. F. W. H. Myers devoted himself.

In a series of four Papers published in the "Proceedings" of the Society, Mr. Myers led the way to the great conclusion at which he gradually arrived. Slightly adapting his words, this conclusion may be thus stated:—That the stream of consciousness in which we habitually live is not the only consciousness which exists in connection with us. Our habitual consciousness may consist of a mere selection from a multitude of thoughts and sensations. Our ordinary waking self has shown itself the fittest to meet the needs of common life. But other thoughts, feelings, and memories, either isolated or in continuous connection, may form a part of our total individuality. It is possible that at some future time, under other conditions, the whole may be recollected, and that the various personalities may be assumed and combined under one single consciousness, in which the consciousness which at this moment directs our actions may be only one element out of many.* This series of articles was published in the " Proceedings " in the years 1884 to 1889, and occupies 160 pages.† In 1892, Mr. Myers commenced the publication of a second series, under the title of "The Subliminal Self." These appeared in the years 1892 to 1895, and comprise nine chapters occupying no fewer than 616 pages.‡

In further explanation of his hypothesis, Mr. Myers says :—

" I suggest that each of us is in reality an abiding psychical entity far more extensive than he knows—an individuality which can never express itself completely through any corporeal manifestation. The Self manifests through the organism ; but there is always some part of the Self unmanifested ; and always, as it seems, some power of organic expression in abeyance or in reserve. Neither can the player express all his thought upon the instrument, nor is the instrument so arranged that all its keys can be sounded at once. One melody after another may be played upon it ; nay— as with the message of duplex or of multiplex telegraphy—simultaneously, or with imperceptible intermissions several melodies can be played together ; but there are still unexhausted reserves of instrumental capacity, as well as unexpressed treasures of informing thought. All this psychical action, I hold, is conscious; all is included in an actual or potential memory below the threshold of our habitual consciousness. For all which lies below that threshold *subliminal* seems the fittest word. ' Unconsciousness,' or even ' Subconscious, ' would be directly misleading ; and to speak (as is sometimes convenient) of the *secondary* self, may give the impression either that there cannot be more selves than two, or that the *superaliminal* self, the self above the threshold—the *empirical* self, the self of common experience— is in some way superior to other possible selves." §

Among undeveloped and unrecognized faculties which, from this point of view, may be looked upon as manifestations of the " Subliminal Self " may be enumerated automatic writing speaking and drawing, crystal-gazing, some dreams and clairvoyant visions, and the means by which various forms of suggestion are carried into effect. Of these faculties, that of automatic writing appears to be

---

* Proceedings, S.P.R., vol. vii. p. 301.

† Proceedings, S.P.R., vol. ii. p. 217, vol. iii. p. i., vol. iv. p. 209, vol. v. p. 522.

‡ Proceedings, S.P.R., vol. vii. p. 298, vol. viii. pp. 333 and 436, vol. ix. p. 3, vol. xi. p. 334.

§ Proceedings, S.P.R., vol. vii. p. 305.

at the present time by far the easiest of exercise and development. A comparatively small amount of patience and perseverance would probably enable a large proportion of persons to practise it. It has, however, its dangerous side, and it should never be taken up without caution, especially by young persons of a sensitive or imaginative turn of mind. It possesses a fascination which, if not controlled, is a temptation to excess, and there is danger of too great an importance being attached to the matter which is written, and of a morbid state of mind being induced.

Automatic speaking has existed, and does now exist, to a much greater extent than is generally supposed to be the case. Some of the preaching and exhortation among the smaller religious sects has probably been of this character. Especially was this so among the Quakers. The perfect silence in which the greater portion of their religious meetings used to be passed in former times, and the entire absence of pre-arrangement, were conditions eminently adapted for the exercise of a "gift" of this kind. It is not surprising that addresses thus given, were attributed to the direct influence of the Holy Spirit on the individual soul. The character and style of preaching which was common among the Quakers until about half a century ago, was frequently on a much higher plane than the speaker seemed capable of in his ordinary moments. In the same way, much of the matter of present-day automatic writing and speaking is apparently above the level of the ordinary powers of the individual. Automatic speaking, at the present time, exists mainly among the "spiritualists," especially in the north of England. It is by them ascribed to the direct control of spirits, generally those of deceased friends.

One of the most remarkable "automatic" speakers, to use the language of Psychical Research, or "inspirational mediums," to use the language of spiritualism, is Mr. J. J. Morse, with whom the writer has been personally acquainted during nearly the whole of his career. J. J. Morse was the son of a well-to-do London publican. At the age of four, his mother died. When he was between eight and nine his father died, having in the meantime lost all his money. He was placed under the care of a woman "whose chief inspiration was the spirit-bottle, and her mode of education was the cane." He ran away, and before he had turned ten years of age was thrown on his own resources, having had six months schooling up to that time, and none subsequently. In his fourteenth year he was in the forecastle of a collier trading between Whitby and

London. Meeting with a severe accident he was discharged, and found himself in London with sixpence in his pocket. For six months he was in the Infirmary of a London Workhouse. On his recovery he got work in some dining-rooms, and in one or two public-houses. Some curious circumstances led him to attend a spiritualistic séance. Soon after this he had his first experience in automatic writing. He was at his work cleaning pewter pots with moist sand, when his finger began writing in the sand, and the words " your mother " were scrawled. He soon got connected sentences written with a pencil, and before long found himself speaking automatically. About this time, James Burns, then the leading spiritualistic bookseller in London, met with him, and gave him permanent employment. His progress after this was sure and steady, and for the last fifteen or twenty years his power of speaking has gained him world-wide renown. When in the United States on a professional engagement he became a member of the American Branch of the Society of Psychical Research. But it is a matter of regret that his experiences have not received any study from the Society in England.

The faculties of automatic speaking and writing must not be confounded with, nor deemed identical with, the facility of extempore speaking or preaching, or of rapid writing, which can be gained by practice, after definite study of a subject, or meditation on a text. It may be difficult in all cases to draw a line, but one is the result of definite intellectual effort, and the other is, so to speak, intuitive. Automatic writing and speaking are often performed in a state of entire unconsciousness, as far as the ordinary senses are concerned. These remarks on automatic speaking and writing are not intended to imply that communications are not thus received from other personalities or from a supernormal source. Mr. Myers himself came to the conclusion that there were cases which could not otherwise be explained. This, however, belongs to a later branch of our subject. But it can hardly fail to be apparent to any one who gives much study to these phenomena, that a different origin must be sought for much that is thus given through the hand and voice.

It is possible, and from one point of view it is very reasonable, to suppose that the faculty of automatic writing and speaking, in the " medium," may present to an outside intelligence, conditions which afford an easier means of communication than the ordinary organs of sense. But the answer to the question, as to whether other personalities have to do with what is spoken or written, must be determined by the matter communicated.

Those who are acquainted with the tone of thought with regard to occult phenomena which prevailed twenty years ago, will realize the great change which has taken place, both among the general public and among spiritualists. This has been mainly due to the work of the Society for Psychical Research, and within the Society, has been mainly due to the work of Mr. Myers. Where there was chaos and a jungle, in which it seemed as though fact and fiction were inextricably and hopelessly intermixed, order and system and law are now becoming visible. To what extent the ultimate solution will identify itself with a " Subliminal Self," in the form in which Mr. Myers has sketched it, it is too early yet to express any confident opinion. Mr. Myers himself would be the last to wish to ascribe finality to any views he put forth. What he said has, as yet, received little attention from leading minds outside his co-workers. In the meantime, the following remarks of two of these—Professor William James, a former President of the Society, and Sir Oliver Lodge, F.R.S., its present President—may be interesting. After narrating some of his own experiences in endeavouring to induce certain of his friends to give some heed to phenomena outside their previous studies, Professor William James says :—

" I should not indulge in the personality and triviality of such anecdotes, were it not that they paint the temper of our time, a temper which, thanks to Frederic Myers more than to any one, will certainly be impossible after this generation. . . . Myer's great principle of research was, that in order to understand any one species of fact we ought to have the species of the same general class of fact before us. So he took a lot of scattered phenomena, some of them recognised as reputable, others outlawed from science, or treated as isolated curiosities ; he made series of them, filled in the transitions by delicate hypotheses or analogies, and bound them together in a system by his bold inclusive conception of the Subliminal Self, so that no one can now touch one part of the fabric without finding the rest entangled with it. Such vague terms of apperception as psychologists have hitherto been satisfied with using for most of these phenomena, as ' fraud,' ' rot,' ' rubbish,' will no more be possible hereafter, than ' dirt ' is possible as a head of classification in chemistry, or ' vermin ' in zoology. Whatever they are, they are things with a right of definite description and to careful observation· . . . Myers' conception of the extensiveness of the Subliminal Self quite overturns the classic notion of what the human mind consists in. The Supraliminal region, as Myers calls it, . . figures in his theory as only a small segment of the psychic spectrum. It is a special phase . evolved for adaptation to our natural environment, and forms only what he calls a privileged case' of personality.    The outlying Subliminal, according to him, represents more fully our central and abiding being.    I think the words subliminal and supraliminal unfortunate, but they were probably unavoidable. I think, too, that Myers's belief in the ubiquity and great extent of the Subliminal will demand a far larger number of facts than sufficed to persuade him, before the next generation of psychologists shall become persuaded. . . What is the precise constitution of the Subliminal ?—Such is the problem which deserves to figure in our Science hereafter as the problem of Myers. . . But Myers has not only propounded the problem definitely, he has also invented definite methods for its solution.    Post-hypnotic suggestion, crystal-gazing, automatic writing and trance-speech, the willing-game, &c., are now, thanks to him, instruments of research . . so many ways of putting the Subliminal on tap."

\*

" Meanwhile, descending to detail, one cannot help admiring the great originality with which Myers wove such an extraordinarily detached and discontinuous series of phenomena together.    Unconscious cerebration, dreams, hypnotism, hysteria, inspirations of genius, the willing-game, planchette, crystal-gazing, hallucinatory voices, apparitions of the dying, medium-trances, démoniacal possession, clairvoyance, thought-transference— even ghosts and other facts more doubtful—these things form a chaos at first sight most discouraging.    No wonder that Scientists can think of no other principle of unity among them than their common appeal to men's perverse propensity to superstition.    Yet Myers has actually made a system of them stringing them continuously upon a perfectly legitimate objective hypothesis verified in some cases, and extended to others by analogy." *

Sir Oliver Lodge says :—

" For that is what Frederic Myers was really doing, all through this last quarter of a century.    He was laying the foundation for a cosmic philosophy, a scheme of existence as large and comprehensive and well founded as any that has appeared. . . A wilderness of facts must be known to all philosophers ; the philosopher is he who recognises their underlying principle and sees the unity running through them all. . . Fifty years ago the facts even of hypnotism were not by orthodox science accepted ; such studies as were made were made almost surreptitiously, here and there, by some truth-seeker clear-sighted enough to outstep the fashion of his time and look at things with his own eyes.    But only with difficulty could he publish his observations, and doubtless many were lost for fear of ridicule and the contempt of his professional brethren.    But now it is different : not so different as it ought to be even yet ; but facts previously considered occult are now investigated and recorded and published in every country of Europe:

* Proceedings, S.P.R., vol. xvii. pp. 15-18, Professor Wm. James. " In Memory of F. W. H. Myers."

. . I claim for Myers that . . he has laid a foundation        on
ground more solid than has ever been available before." *

Besides his share in " Phantasms of the Living" and the Papers
published in the " Proceedings" of the Society, Mr. Myers left
behind him an uncompleted work entitled " Human Personality and
its Survival of Bodily Death." This work has been brought out
under the editorship of Dr. Richard Hodgson and Miss Alice Johnson,
and contains his last words on the Subliminal Self.    In an
announcement respecting it, it was stated :—

" This work aims at presenting in continuous form the bulk of the
evidence, experimental and otherwise, which points to human faculty
operating below the threshold of ordinary consciousness during the life of
earth, and to human faculty continuing to operate after the body's decay.
Among the subjects treated of in this book are Alternating Personalities,
Hysteria, Genius, Sleep, Dreams, Hypnotism, Apparitions, Crystal-Gazing,
Automatic Writing, Trance, Possession, Ecstasy, Life after Death."

This chapter on the work of the Society is necessarily more
intimately associated than any other with the name of Mr. Myers.

---

* Proceedings, S.P.R., vol. xvii. pp. 2-4. Sir Oliver Lodge.    "In
Memory of F. W. H. Myers."

# CHAPTER V.

## Apparitions and Hauntings.

### I.—Apparitions.

IN 1886, four years after the establishment of the Society, a large work before alluded to was published in two volumes, under the title of "Phantasms of the Living." The authors' names on the title page are Edmund Gurney, F. W. H. Myers, and F. Podmore. For some years it has been out of print, and second hand copies are obtainable only at a price considerably above the original cost. The Preface says that a large part of the material used in the book was sent to the authors as representatives of the Society for Psychical Research, and that the book was published with the sanction of the Council of the Society. In the Introduction, for which Mr. Myers is solely responsible, he says:—

"The subject of this book is one which a brief title is hardly sufficient to explain. For under our heading of "Phantasms of the Living" we propose, in fact, to deal with all classes of cases where there is reason to suppose that the mind of one human being has affected the mind of another, without speech uttered, or word written, or sign made ; has affected it, that is to say, by other means than through the recognised channels of sense.

. But for reasons which will be made manifest as we proceed, we have included among telepathic phenomena a vast class of cases which seem at first sight to involve something widely different from a mere transference of thought. I refer to apparitions, excluding indeed the alleged apparitions of the dead, but including the apparitions of all persons who are still living, as we know life, though they may be on the very brink and border of physical dissolution."*

Seven hundred and two numbered cases are described in the book. In all of them, selected from the far larger number which were presented to the Society, the evidence was considered sufficiently strong to warrant belief in the reality of the phenomena. About 400 out of the 700 are classed as Visual, that is, as apparitions in

* " Phantasms of the Living," vol. I. Intro. p. xxxv.

the ordinary sense of the word, the main feature of which is generally a figure. Space will permit of four cases only being referred to as illustrations, the original reports being necessarily condensed.

No. 163.—From the Rev. W. J. Ball, of 6, Pemberton Terrace, Cambridge.—"During my college days I had a very dear and intimate chum, R. F. Dombrain. . . We hoped to go together into the foreign mission field.      . He was seized with a very bad fever. . . At last he recovered and returned to Dublin. . . This was the state of things when I went down to the County Limerick in the spring of 1853. . . Letters from my friend told me of gradually improving health. . . I felt perfectly at ease about my dear friend's recovery. . . On the morning of the 14th of April, I had the most vivid dream I remember ever to have seen. I seemed to be walking with young Dombrain, amidst some beautiful scenery, when suddenly I was brought to a waking condition by a sort of light appearing before me. I started up in my bed, and saw before me, in his ordinary dress and appearance, my friend, who seemed to be passing from earth towards the light above. He seemed to give me one loving smile, and I felt that his look contained an expression of affectionate separation and farewell. Then I leaped out of bed, and cried with a loud voice : 'Robert, Robert,' and the vision was gone. .      I looked at my watch and found the time three minutes past five. . . I wrote to my sister asking for particulars, and for the exact time the death had taken place. Never once did the slightest doubt cross my mind that my friend had died. The following morning I received a letter from my sister, stating that . . . at 3 minutes past 5 in the morning he had quietly passed away from this world."[*]

No. 207.—From Mrs. Larcombe, 8, Runton Street, Hornsey Rise, London, N.—"When I was about 18 or 19, I went to stay in Guernsey. This would be about 30 years ago. About 10 a.m. one day, I was sitting in the kitchen, blowing up the fire with the bellows. I heard some very beautiful music, and stopped to listen, at the same time looking up. I saw above me thousands of angels, as tight as they could be packed, seeming to rise far above and beyond me. They were only visible as far as the head and shoulders. In front of them all, I saw my friend Anne Cox. As I looked and listened, the music seemed to die away in the distance, and at the same time, the angels seemed to pass away into the distance, and vanish like smoke. I ran up to Miss White, the young lady staying in the house, and told her what I had seen. She said, 'You may be sure your friend Anne Cox has gone to Heaven.' I wrote home at once to Lyme Regis, and found that Anne Cox had died that very day. She and I had been very close friends. She was just my own age, and was almost like a sister to me."—Mrs. Larcombe states positively that she was in no anxiety about her friend, and had no knowledge of her illness."[†]

[*] "Phantasms of the Living," vol. I. pp. 417-18.

[†] "Phantasms of the Living," vol. I. p. 552.

No. 212.—From Rowland Bowstead, M.D., Caistor.—"In September, 1847, I was playing in a cricket match. . . A ball was driven in my direction, . . and rolled towards a low hedge. I and another lad ran after it. When I got near the hedge, I saw the apparition of my half-brother, who was much endeared to me, over the hedge, dressed in a shooting suit with a gun on his arm ; he smiled and waved his hand at me. I called the attention of the other boy to the same, but when we looked again the figure had vanished. I, feeling very sad at the time, went up to my uncle, and told him of what I had seen. He took out his watch and noted the time, just 10 minutes to one o'clock. Two days after I received a letter from my father, informing me of the death of my half-brother, John Mounsey, which took place (at Lincoln) at 10 minutes to 1. His death was singular, for on that morning he said he was much better, and thought he should be able to shoot again. Taking up his gun, he turned round to my father, asking him if he had sent for me, as he particularly wished to see me. I was a great favourite of his. My father replied the distance was too far, and expense to great to send for me, it being over 100 miles. At this he put himself into a passion, and said he would see me in spite of them all, for he did not care for expense or distance. Suddenly a blood vessel on his lungs burst, and he died at once. He was at the time dressed in a shooting suit, and had his gun on his arm. I knew he was ill, but . . he was improving. . . His disease was consumption."[*]

No. 242.—From Mrs. Clerke, Clifton Lodge, Farquhar Road, Upper Norwood, London, S.E.—"In the month of August, 1864, about 3 or 4 o'clock in the afternoon, I was sitting reading in the verandah of our house in Barbadoes. My black nurse was driving my little girl, about 18 months or so old, in her perambulator in the garden. I got up after some time to go into the house not having noticed anything at all, when this black woman said to me. 'Missis, who was that gentleman that was talking to you just now?' 'There was no one talking to me,' I said. 'Oh yes, dere was, Missis, a very pale gentleman, very tall, and he talked to you, and you was very rude, for you never answered him.' I repeated there was no one, and got rather cross with the woman, and she begged me to write down the day, for she knew she had seen some one. I did, and in a few days I heard of the death of my brother in Tobago. Now the curious part is this, that I did not see him, but she—a stranger to him—did, and she said that he seemed very anxious for me to notice him."[†]

In answer to enquiries, Mrs. Clerke added that the day of death was the same, for she wrote it down. The description, "very tall and pale," was accurate. She had no idea that he was ill. The woman had never seen him. She had been with Mrs. Clerke about 18 months, and had no object in telling her. Colonel Clerke, Mrs. Clerke's husband, writes that he well remembers the incident of his wife's brother, Mr. John Beresford, dying in Tobago, and the black nurse's declaration that she saw, as nearly as possible

---

[*] "Phantasms of the Living," vol. I. p. 560.

[†] "Phantasms of the Living," vol. II. p. 61.

at the time of his death, a gentleman exactly answering to Mr. Beresford's description leaning over the back of Mrs. Clerke's easy-chair in the open verandah.

A single instance of an apparition from the later records of the Society must suffice. It is one that possesses several characteristics of special and almost unique interest. It is quite recent. So recent, in fact, that the real names of persons and localities cannot be given, and some details have to be omitted. The case is reported at length in the " Proceedings" of the Society, vol. xi., pp. 547 to 559. Mr. Myers, of one of whose articles it forms a part, states that the true names are all known to him, and he vouches for the accuracy of the story. The following are its principal features :—

Mrs. Claughton, a widow lady, moving in good society, has had several experiences of apparitions. True statements have thus been made to her, but she had not paid much attention to them nor sought to encourage them. She endeavoured to keep the present adventure quiet, but vague and distorted versions of it got about, so that she consented to give to the Marquis of Bute, and through him to the Society, her own account of such incidents as she did not, for the sake of those still living, feel bound to conceal. On the occasion of a visit to a house in London reputed to be haunted she twice saw a phantasm—a figure of a lady unknown to her, and who made many statements of facts unknown to her. Some of these which could be at once verified were found to be correct. On the second occasion the figure of a man was also present—"tall, dark, well-made, healthy, 60 years old or more, ordinary man's day clothes, kind good expression." A long conversation ensued between the three, in the course of which the following statements and requests were made :—The man stated himself to be George Howard, buried in Meresby churchyard, and gave the dates of his marriage and death. He desired Mrs. Claughton to go to Meresby to verify these dates in the registers and then to go to the church at the ensuing 1.15 a.m., and wait at the grave therein (S.W. corner of aisle) of Richard Hart, giving his age and date of death. She was to verify this also in the registers. The place and these persons were quite unknown to Mrs. Claughton. The apparition of the man then proceeded to tell her various circumstances that would occur. Her railway ticket would not be taken. She was to send it along with a white rose from his grave to Dr. Ferrier. Joseph Wright, a dark man, would help her. She would lodge with a woman who would tell her that a child of her own, who had been drowned, was buried in the same churchyard. She was told that when she had done all this she would receive further information.

The next morning Mrs. Claughton sent for Dr. Ferrier, who corroborated certain facts within his knowledge. From the Post Office she found that Meresby existed, and was an obscure country village four or five hours' railway journey from London. Mrs. Claughton arranged to go to Meresby the next Saturday afternoon. On the Friday night previously she dreamt that there was a fair going on, and that she had to go to place after place to get lodgings. All this proved to be the case, but she finally took lodgings at the house of Joseph Wright, who turned out to be the parish clerk. In the confusion of her arrival at the railway station her ticket had not been asked for. The same evening she sent to the curate (the rector being oft duty from age) as to consulting registers. He was dining out, and was unable to see her that night, but sent word that he would be happy for her to see the registers after Sunday morning service. On Sunday morning Mrs. Wright talked to her about her drowned child buried in the church-yard. She went to the morning service, and immediately afterwards went into the vestry and verified the registers. She described George Howard to Joseph Wright, and he showed her his grave and that of Richard Hart. On the former there was no stone, but the grave was surrounded by a railing overgrown with white roses. She gathered one for Dr. Ferrier as directed. She had a walk and talk with the curate, " who was not sympa-thetic." He declined to assist her any further, but told the parish clerk he could do as he liked as to admitting the lady to the church that night. The clerk agreed to do as Mrs. Claughton desired. He called her at a quarter to one o'clock in the morning, and took her to the church. They searched the interior and found it empty. In the statement which Mrs. Claughton placed in the hands of the Marquis of Bute she says that at 1.20 a.m. she was locked in the church alone, having no light. She waited near the grave of Richard Hart. She felt no fear. She received a communication, no details of which she feels free to give, but the history which was begun in London was completed. She was directed to take another white rose from George Howard's grave and give it personally to his unmarried daughter living at Hart Hall, and to remark her likeness to him. About 1.45 Joseph Wright knocked and let Mrs. Claughton out. She went to George Howard's grave and gathered a rose for Miss Howard as directed. She then went to bed and slept well for the first time since the first appearance of the apparition.

The following is a copy of a Memorandum made by Mrs. Claughton previous to the journey, the original of which was seen by Mr. Myers. He was fully satisfied as to its genuineness:—

" Go to Meresby. Railway ticket not asked for. Porter to have one of K.'s names. Ask for marriage register of George Howard. Find out last day the name Mrs. T. Find grave in churchyard with white roses. Send white rose to Dr. Ferrier. Ask on arrival at Meresby for Mr. Francis. Dark man, Wright—big, fresh-coloured, healthy fellow—will help me in what I have to do. Find grave of Richard Hart in church. Verify home of Mr. Howard. Verify village—village fair going on. Church standing away far by itself. Stay in house of woman whose boy is buried in same churchyard as Mr. Howard. Watch in church by Mr. Hart's grave. Dark man—Wright—to take me there."[*]

[*]Proceedings, S.P.R., vol. xi. p. 553.

The following are notes by Mr. Myers on this Memorandum. As to the third sentence, "*i.e.*, to have as a surname the Christian name of one of Mrs. Claughton's daughters—which turned out to be the case" "The gentleman so designated (Mr. Francis) was concerned in the private matters ; was found as predicted." "There was a fair going on in Meresby, as predicted." "Found true" (church standing by itself). "Found when in house that boy was so buried."[*]

In the report of this case in the "Proceedings" of the S.P.R., where it occupies twelve pages, several confirmatory statements and letters are given, including one by Mr. Andrew Lang, who received a narrative written out partly by Dr. Ferrier and partly by Mrs. Ferrier. Dr. Ferrier is connected as trustee with the house in which Mrs. Claughton saw the apparitions.

## II.—Hauntings.

"Hauntings" may conveniently be described as phenomena which appear to be attached to particular localities, and include apparitions as well as sights and sounds of various character. The records of the Society contain descriptions of a large number of cases in which the evidence of the reality of phenomena incapable of ordinary explanation is absolutely conclusive. The most remarkable of the "haunted house" cases is given at length, under the title, "Record of a Haunted House, by Miss Morton,"[†] For various reasons it was needful that the real name of the family should be considered private, the name Morton is therefore substituted, but with that exception the names and initials are the true ones. The followin is an outline of the principal features of the story :—

The house is an ordinary detached modern residence, standing in its own gardens, and separated from a road in front by railings and a short carriage drive. It was built about 1860. For a period of seven years, from 1882 to 1889, the hauntings continued, the most frequent phenomenon being the appearance of the figure of a lady, both in the house and in the garden The house, during this period, was occupied by persons described as Captain and Mrs. Morton and their family, consisting of four unmarried daughters and two sons. The eldest daughter, aged 19 in 1882, was the chief percipient and the chief narrator. She was a young lady of a scientific turn of mind, and has been educated for the medical profession. She

[*] Proceedings, S.P.R., vol. xi. p. 553.
[†] Proceedings, S.P.R., vol. viii. pp. 311-332.

describes a number of occasions when she saw the figure in the passages, on the stairs, in various rooms, and in the garden. It was also seen by other members of the family, by visitors, and by servants, altogether by at least twenty different persons. The appearance of the figure seemed to identify it with a former resident in the house, with whose history and death some tragic circumstances were connected. Varying kinds of footsteps were also heard, and heavy thuds and other noises. Lights were also occasionally seen, and "a cold wind" felt. The following paragraphs are quoted from an account furnished by Miss Morton :—

### "PROOFS OF IMMATERIALITY [OF THE FIGURE].

"1.—I have several times fastened fine strings across the stairs at various heights before going to bed, but after all others have gone up to their rooms. These were fastened in the following way : I made small pellets of marine glue, into which I inserted the ends of the cord, then stuck one pellet lightly against the wall and the other to the bannister, the string being thus stretched across the stairs. They were knocked down by a very slight touch, and yet would not be felt by anyone passing up or down the stairs, and by candle-light could not be seen from below. They were put up at various heights from the ground, from six inches to the height of the bannisters—about three feet. I have twice at least seen the figure pass through the cords, leaving them intact.

"2.—The sudden and complete disappearance of the figure while still in full view."

"3.—The impossibility of touching the figure. I have repeatedly followed it into a corner, when it disappeared, and have tried to suddenly pounce upon it, but have never succeeded in touching it or getting my hand up to it, the figure eluding my touch.

"It has appeared in a room with the doors shut."*

Miss Morton also says :—"The figure is undoubtedly connected with the house, none of the percipients having seen it anywhere else, nor had any other hallucination."†

Separate accounts by six other persons are also given. The figure was several times seen in broad daylight. The complicity of servants seems excluded for various reasons, one being that all were changed during the time the occurrences took place. The article in the "Proceedings" is illustrated by three plans showing the rooms where the figure was seen, and the different courses it took. Mr. Myers makes this comment after interviewing several of the percipients :—"It is observable that the phenomena, as seen or

* Proceedings, S.P.R., vol. viii. p. 321, 322.
† Proceedings, S.P.R., vol. viii. p. 322.

heard by all the witnesses, are very uniform in character—even in the numerous instances where there had been no previous communication between the percipients."* From 1887 to 1889 the figure was very seldom seen, and the louder noises had gradually ceased. The lighter footsteps lasted a little longer, but no occurrences have since been observed. Numbers of cases of an analogous character furnish evidence of the reality of facts which it seems impossible to explain away; but no other case presents such a mass of unimpeachable testimony from such a variety of persons. So that the position seems amply justified, that whatever may be the explanation, the phenomena are real and cannot be accounted for by any recognised cause.

# CHAPTER VI.

## Evidence of the Existence of Intelligences other than "The Living," and of the Reality of Inter-communication.

WB have now reached the last of the branches of the work of the Society as enumerated in the opening chapter, and that one on which the supreme interest of these enquiries centres :—Are there other intelligences than those which we see around us in the flesh, and, if so, is inter-communication possible?

It may be worth while, for a few moments, to look at this question from the point of view of analogy. We look around us on this earth, and we find what is to us an infinite variety of animal life, from the most minute microscopical forms up to man. It is foreign to our purpose to enquire whether these constitute an unbroken series; but it is clear that most or all of this life is accompanied with more or less intelligence, again varying in amount to an infinite degree. It would be presumptuous in us to imagine, especially in view of recent developments of physical science, and of recent investigations into the powers of the human mind, that man, with his five senses, is conscious of, or is capable of perceiving, all forms of intelligent life connected with this earth The presumption is quite the other way. Analogy would lead us to infer the probability that the range and amount of life on the earth is far greater than we know. Then, again, if we extend our vision, and regard this earth as a small globe, one amid myriads of others apparently similarly constituted, we can hardly avoid the conclusion that it is infinitely improbable that the earth is the only body in the material universe which is a home of intelligent life All this, however, only leads us towards the great question,— "When a man dies, does he live again?" Does analogy give us any help here? We fear the answer must be—"It does not." We search into and we question Nature, as we know it, in vain for any indication that any single individual living thing continues a separate existence after material death. For an answer to that question, or for any evidence of such continued existence, we must either go into another kingdom, or we must widely extend our conceptions of Nature. A double problem thus presents itself to the psychical enquirer—(1), Are there intelligent beings around us, of whom we are not ordinarily conscious; (2), if so, who and what are they, and are any or all of them human beings, who have passed through the change we call death, still living on under other conditions?

The extent to which the latent and undeveloped powers of the mind are capable of accounting for the great mass of phenomena which confront us in psychical investigation, is a question beset with difficulties and complications. It is a scientific duty to exhaust all known and recognised causes to the utmost reasonable extent before admitting the influence of other intelligent beings. The records of the Society contain much valuable matter showing how far argument can be pushed, and facts interpreted, without such an admission. Many of the leading workers in the Society have, however, been driven to the conclusion that certain facts do exist, which cannot be explained without admitting the presence of other intelligences, and that some of these facts are evidence of the continued action of men and women who have lived among us.

The limits of this chapter will admit of the citation of four instances only, in which the evidence of the continued action of a deceased person is so strong as to have brought conviction to many minds.

I. ABRAHAM FLORENTINE.*—The Medium in this case was the Rev. W. Stainton Moses, M.A. (Oxon). He was one of the original members of the Council of the Society, and occupied an important scholastic position. In August, 1874, he was staying with his friends, Dr. and Mrs. Speer, at Shanklin, in the Isle of Wight. The three were seated round a heavy loo table. It began to "tilt" in a very violent manner. A message was spelt out purporting to come from Abraham Florentine stating that he had died at Brooklyn, New York, on the 5th of that month in that year. He further said he was in the War of 1812; and the words, "a month and 17 days" were added. These were afterwards found to refer to his own age when he died, being that much over 83 years. Enquiries were instituted. The Military Authorities of New York State reported that Abraham Florentine was a private in a regiment of New York Militia, and served in the War referred to. Dr. Eugene Crowell,

* Proceedings, S.P.R., vol. xi. pp. 82-85.

of Brooklyn, undertook to make further enquiries. In a letter dated February 15th, 1875, he says that in the Directory he found the name of Abraham Florentine. On calling at the address given, he met a very respectable elderly lady, with whom the following conversation ensued :—

"Q. Does Mr. Abraham Florentine reside here ?—A. He did reside here but is dead now.

"Q. May I enquire whether you are Mrs. Florentine, his widow?—A. I am.

"Q. May I ask when he died ?—A. Last August.

"Q. At what time in the month ?—A. On the 5th.

"Q. What was his age at time of decease ?—A. 83.

"Q. Did he pass his 83rd year ?—A. Yes, his 83rd birthday was the previous 8th of June.

"Q. Was he engaged in any war ?—A. Yes. In the war of 1812."

Mr. W. Stainton Moses, commenting on this, says :—

"Most undoubtedly, none of us had ever heard of Abraham Florentine, nor had any of us friends in America who could have given us news of what went on there.    . As a plain matter of truth, I repeat that both names and facts were entirely unknown to us."

Mr. F. W. H. Myers investigated this case, and considered its evidential value justified him in including it in one of his articles on the experiences of Mr. W. Stainton Moses.

II.  ONE OF MRS. PIPER'S "CONTROLS." — The Trance Experiences of Mrs. Piper have attracted very wide attention. On no single investigation has anything like an equal amount of time and labour been bestowed. Four elaborate Records of Observations have been published by the Society, occupying in all over 1300 pages in the "Proceedings,"* besides various articles on the case of a critical character. One of the most distinct and interesting of the many personalities which have professed to manifest through Mrs. Piper is that of "George Pelham" (not the real name), designated for brevity's sake "G. P." He was a young man of good education who was associated with Dr. Richard Hodgson, the Secretary of the American Branch of S.P.R., in the investigation of Mrs. Piper. He lost his life suddenly by an accident—and, a few weeks later, communications commenced to come through Mrs. Piper, pro-

* Proceedings, S.P.R., vol. vi. (Part xvii) pp. 436-659.—vol. viii. (Part xxi) pp. 1-167.—vol. xiii (Part xxxii) pp. 284-582.—vol. xvi (Part xli.) pp. 1-649.

fessing to be fro him. Dr. Hodgson devotes 40 pages in one of his Reports a "History of the 'G. P.' communications." In g up the effect on his own mind, Dr. Hodgson says :—

"Finally, the manifestations of this G.P. communicating have not been of a fitful and spasmodic nature, they have exhibited the marks of a continuous living and persistent personality, manifesting itself through a course of years, and showing the same characteristics of an independent intelligence whether friends of G.P. were present at the sitting or not. I learned of various cases where, in my absence, active assistance was rendered by G.P. to sitters who had never previously heard of him, and from time to time he would make brief pertinent reference to matters with which G.P. living was acquainted, though I was not, and sometimes in ways which indicated that he could to some extent see what was happening in our world to persons in whose welfare G.P. living would have been specially interested."*

In a later portion of the same Report, speaking of G.P. and other communicators, Dr. Hodgson says :—

"What my future beliefs may be, I do not know. . It may be that further experiment in the lines of investigation before us may lead me to change my view ; but at the present time I cannot profess to have any doubt but that the chief 'communicators' to whom I have referred in the foregoing pages are veritably the personalities that they claim to be, that they have survived the change we call death, and that they have directly communicated with us, whom we call living, through Mrs. Piper's entranced organism."†

Before proceeding to the third case it may be interesting to quote a few words from the last published Report on Mrs. Piper by Prof. J. H. Hyslop, Ph.D., of Columbia University, New York :—

"If I had to judge the case by my own experiments and record alone, I do not see how I could avoid the conclusion that a future life is absolutely demonstrated by them."‡

III. ONE OF MRS. THOMPSON'S "CONTROLS."—Mrs. Thompson is a lady moving in middle-class society in London, whose "mediumship" is of a similar kind to that of Mrs. Piper. She has for some years been a member of the Society for Psychical Research, and has kindly allowed many of its leading members to have sittings with her. Only one Report respecting these has yet appeared. It is contained in the current volume of the "Proceedings," and includes an article by Mr. Myers, one of the last he wrote. He sat with her many times. He says:—"I believe that most of these messages are uttered through Mrs. Thompson's organism by spirits who for the time inform or 'possess' that organism."§ The

---

* Proceedings, S.P.R., vol. xiii. p. 330.
† Proceedings, S.P.R., vol. xiii. pp. 405-6.
‡ Proceedings, S.P R., vol. xvi. p. 242.
§ Proceedings, S.P.R., vol. xvii. p. 73.

special case selected for quotation is described in an article by Dr. F. Van Eeden, of Bussum, Holland. The substance of it was read at a meeting of the Society on April 19th, 1901. Referring to his visits to Mrs. Thompson in November and December, 1899, and in June, 1900, Dr. Van Eeden says:—

" I brought a piece of clothing that had belonged to a young man who had committed suicide. Nobody in the world knew that I had kept it, nor that I had taken it to England with me for this purpose, and yet I got an exact description of the young man and the manner of his suicide, and even his Christian name was given," *

Dr. Van Eeden proceeds to discuss the possible telepathic explanation. Again, he says :—

" Up to the sitting of June 7th [1900], all the information came through Nelly, Mrs. Thompson's so-called spirit-control. But on that date the deceased tried, as he had promised, to take the control himself, as the technical term goes. The evidence then became very striking. During a few minutes—though a few minutes only— I felt absolutely as if I were speaking to my friend himself. I spoke Dutch, and got immediate and correct answers. The expression of satisfaction and gratification in face and gesture, when we seemed to understand each other, was too true and vivid to be acted. Quite unexpected Dutch words were pronounced, details were given which were far from my mind, some of which I had never known, and found to be true only on enquiry afterwards." †

In concluding his article Dr. Van Eeden says :—

"And here, I think, I may make a definite and clear statement of my present opinion, which has been wavering between the two sides for a long time. I should not give any definite statement if I did not feel prepared to do so, however eagerly it might be desired, for I think it the first duty of a scientist and philosopher to abstain from definite statements in uncertain matters. And in observations like these we must reckon with a very general inclination to deny, on second thoughts, what seemed absolutely convincing on the spot and at the moment. Every phenomenon or occurrence of a very extraordinary character is only believed after repeated observation. After the first experience one's mind refuses to stay in the unaccustomed channel of thought, and next morning we say :—' I must have been mistaken, I must have overlooked this or that, there must be some ordinary explanation.' But at this present moment it is about eight months since I had my last sitting with Mrs. Thompson, in Paris, and yet when I read the notes again it is impossible for me to abstain from the

* Proceedings, S.P.R., vol. xvii. pp. 77-78.

† Proceedings, S.P.R., vol. xvii. p. 82.

conviction that I have really been a witness, were it only for a few minutes, of the voluntary manifestion of a deceased person."\*

IV.—BLANCHE ABERCROMBY (not real name).†—This is a very curious case. A number of MS. books belonging to Mr. W. Stainton Moses were placed in the hands of Mr. Myers by Mr. Stainton Moses' literary Executors, Mr. C. C. Massey and Mr. Alfred A. Watts. In one of these books were some pages gummed down, apparently by Mr. Stainton Moses, and marked by him " private matter." With the permission of the Executors, Mr. Myers carefully opened the pages. In describing what he found, he says the case " is in some respects the most remarkable of all [among those of alleged spirits whose communications are in any way evidential], from the series of chances which have been needful in order to establish its veracity." Mr. Myers continues :

"The spirit in question is that of a lady known to me, whom Mr. Moses had met, I believe, once only. The lady died on a Sunday afternoon, about 20 years ago, at a country house about 200 miles from London. Her death, which was regarded as a matter of public interest, was at once telegraphed to London, and appeared in Monday's *Times;* but of course, on Sunday evening, no one in London, save the Press and perhaps the immediate family, was cognisant of the fact. On that evening near midnight a communication purporting to come from her was made to Mr. Moses, at his secluded lodgings in the North of London. The identity was some days later corroborated by a few lines purporting to come directly from her, and to be in her handwriting. There is no reason to suppose that Mr. Moses had ever seen this handwriting. . . On receiving these messages he seems to have mentioned them to no one, and simply to have gummed down the pages in his MS. book."

Mr. Myers continues:—

"The book when placed in my hands was still thus gummed down. . . I opened the pages, and was surprised to find a brief letter (automatically written, professedly from Blanche Abercromby), which though containing no definite facts was entirely characteristic of the Blanche Abercromby I had known. But although I had received letters from her in life, I had no recollection of her handwriting. I happened to know a son of hers sufficiently well to be able to ask his aid—aid which, I may add, he would have been most unlikely to afford to a stranger. He lent me a letter for comparison. The strong resemblance was at once obvious, but the A of the surname was made in the letter in a way quite different from that adopted in the automatic script. The son then allowed me to study a long series of letters, reaching

---

\* Proceedings, S.P.R., vol. xvii. pp. 83-84.

† Proceedings, S.P.R., vol. xi. pp. 96-99.

down till almost the date of her death. From these it appeared that during the last year of her life she had taken to writing the A (as her husband had always done) in the way in which it was written in the automatic script. The resemblance of handwriting appeared both to the son and to myself to be incontestable, but as we desired an experienced opinion he allowed me to submit the note-book and two letters to Dr. Hodgson. . . . Dr. Hodgson reports as follows " :—

" I have compared the writing numbered 123 in the note-book of Mr. Stainton Moses with Epistles of Jan. 4th, 18—, and Sep 19th, 18—, written by B.A. The note-book writing bears many minor resemblances to that of the epistles, and there are also several minor differences in the formation of some of the letters, judging at least from the two epistles submitted to me ; but the resemblances are more characteristic than the differences. In addition there are several striking peculiarities common to the epistles and the note-book writing, which appear to be specially emphasized in the latter. The note-book writing suggests that its author was attempting to reproduce the B.A. writing by recalling to memory its chief peculiarities, and not by copying from specimens of the B.A. writing. The signature, especially in the note-book writing, is characteristically like an imitation from memory of B.A.'s signature. I have no doubt whatever that the person who wrote the note-book writing intended to reproduce the writing of B.A.

RICHARD HODGSON.

5, Boylston Place, Boston [U.S.A.], September 4th, 1893."

A postscript to B.A.'s letter in the note-book is in these words :— " It is like my writing as evidence to you." Mr. Myers adds this remark :—

" The chances necessary to secure a verification of this case were more complex than can here be fully explained. This lady, who was quite alien to these researches, had been dead about twenty years when her posthumous letter was discovered in Mr. Moses' private note-book by one of the very few surviving persons who had both known her well enough to recognise the characteristic quality of the message, and were also sufficiently interested in spirit identity to get the handwritings compared and the case recorded."

# CHAPTER VII.

## CONCLUSIONS.

ONE subject—the so-called "Divining" or "Dowsing Rod," has been omitted from the classification of the work of the Society, and yet it cannot be passed over in silence It occupies a unique position. Considerable difference of opinion existed within the Society as to whether it was a matter which properly came within the scope of its enquiries. This, it seems to the writer, can hardly be open to question. It certainly comes within the category of "branches of enquiry which have not received adequate attention from the literary and scientific world." It also possesses considerable psychological as well as practical interest. In 1884, a member of the Society, Mr. E. Vaughan Jenkins, placed at its disposal a valuable collection of contemporary evidence. This, supplemented by further enquiry by Mr. Edward R. Pease, showed that a strong *primâ facie* case for fuller investigation existed.* Accordingly, in 1891, the Council of the Society considered the matter of sufficient importance to request Professor W. F. Barrett, F.R.S., to submit the whole subject to a thorough scientific and experimental research. This proved to be a tedious and laborious undertaking. The two bulky Reports published in the "Proceedings" of the Society† are the outcome of Professor Barrett's indefatigable industry. His labours in regard to them extended over a number of years. Though Professor Barrett's researches have placed the matter in a new light, and have furnished a large mass of sifted evidence, the subject is yet far from exhausted, and the complete ultimate explanation of the very remarkable results obtained, in so many cases, by means of the Rod, is still obscure.

In attempting to sum up the work which the Society for Psychical Research has accomplished during the first twenty years of its existence, it may be claimed:—

---

* Proceedings, S.P.R., vol. ii. (part v.), pp. 79-107.

† Proceedings, S.P.R., vol. xiii. (part xxxii.), pp. 2-282, and vol. xv. (part xxxvi.) pp. 130-383.

(1.) That proof is afforded that there are other means than the "five senses" by which knowledge can be acquired by the human mind; in other words, that Telepathy is a Fact.

(2.) That one human mind has the power of influencing other human minds in ways not heretofore recognized by science; in other words, that the effects of Suggestion, Hypnotism, and Psychic Healing represent groups of actual Phenomena.

(3.) That there is a realm of undeveloped and unrecognized Faculty in Man, provisionally termed the Subliminal Self.

(4.) That there is a basis of fact in many stories of Hauntings and Apparitions of various kinds.

(5.) That in Psychical Research the enquirer does meet with Intelligences other than human beings in the flesh. And that there is evidence—small though it be in amount—which is sufficient to prove the continuity of individual life after death, and that communication does take place between those in this and in another condition of life.

It is claimed that the small selection of evidence presented in the preceding five chapters is sufficient to establish these propositions. Even in regard to the last, the evidence cannot be set aside. If it is ignored, the objector must be prepared to deny the value of human testimony altogether, even if he is not driven to question the objective reality of all external phenomena. In regard to all the departments into which the work of the Society has been divided the mass of evidence presented in its publications is very great compared with the few cases quoted in the preceding pages, some of them only in a condensed form. Take the case of Mrs. Claughton alone. If it is read in its entirety in the "Proceedings," it will be seen that it combines almost every phase of psychical phenomena; and that the quality of the evidence as to the facts is as good as can be desired.

It should always be remembered that the Society comes to no collective conclusions. There has always existed the greatest diversity of view among its members on nearly every branch of investigation. This is likely always to be the case. On the title page of its "Proceedings" this notice appears:—"The responsibility for both the facts and the reasonings in papers published in the 'Proceedings' rests entirely with their authors."

It must also be borne in mind that positive evidence and negative evidence (if the phrase may be allowed) do not stand on the same level.  The Irishman who is said to have brought forward twenty witnesses who did not see him steal the potatoes, to confront the one witness who did, did not help his case.  Failures to obtain or to witness phenomena, and attempts to explain alleged phenomena by hitherto recognized causes, even when successful cannot be allowed to counterbalance positive evidence on the other side, unless all conditions are identical.

There are some suggestive paragraphs by Mr. F. C. S. Schiller, of Oxford, in the current volume of the "Proceedings." They occur in the review of a book by Professor Flournoy, of Geneva.*  Mr. Schiller says:—

" I prefer to preserve an open mind with regard to any explanation that may be propounded, and to leave myself free to hold that the truth will probably turn out to be far greater and more complicated than is as yet anticipated by the rival theorists.    The fact seems to be that spiritists as yet have hardly a notion of the resources which modern psychology and philosophy may yield them for the defence of their favourite thesis, and do not realise how hollow is the ground on which the 'scientific' materialism of their opponents stands.   Materialism has the support (broadly) of our existing academic *personnel*, of the customary ways of common-sense, and of the inertia which shrinks from translating speculation into experimentation.  But all these things are capable of being altered, if a really strong and genuine desire to know can be aroused with regard to these subjects.  But when it is, and when the spiritist theory is advocated by one who really knows where the land lies,  .  .  . the notion of a relation between our world and an 'other,' which should take the form of one in physical space (i.e., in the space of *our* world), will then be seen to possess precisely the same crudeness as the ancients' fancy, that by descending the crater of Avernus one might go straight to the house of Hades, and that by sailing westwards beyond the Pillars of Hercules one might reach the Islands of the Blest.

" From the very nature of the case, the relation between two worlds (*i.e.*, modes of experience) must be of a psychological order.  The alleged 'other' world cannot lie north, east, west, or south of ours.   It must be a state of consciousness, or a mode of experience, into which we pass from that constituting our 'world,' and from which we can, perhaps, repass.  In comprehending its relation to ours, therefore, the guiding analogies must be psychological.    In other words, the relation must be conceived as analogous to that of a 'dream' world to a 'real' world—without of course prejudging the question which is to be regarded as the 'reality' and which as the 'dream.'   That question can only be decided by the comparison of the contents of the two 'worlds,' and (since we *ex hypothesi*

* Proceedings, S.P.R., vol. xvii., pp. 245-251.

start from our world) by the *value* of the revelations of the 'other' world for our life."

The purpose of these pages will have been answered if they draw increased attention to the interest and value of Psychical Enquiry, and if some are thereby induced to study the work and publications of the Society for Psychical Research, with which Society the writer will always consider it one of the greatest privileges of his life to have been associated. The "Proceedings" of the Society are published by R. Brimley Johnson, 8, York Buildings, Adelphi, London, W.C. All information regarding the Society can be obtained from the Secretary, 20, Hanover Square, London, W.

The following lines from Tennyson were quoted by Sir Oliver Lodge, in his Presidential address to the Society, in 1902. They might be headed :—

### PAST—PRESENT—FUTURE.

"Out of the deep, my child, out of the deep,
　From that true world within the world we see,
　Where of our world is but the bounding shore."

\* \* \*

"The Ghost in Man, the Ghost that once was Man,
　But cannot wholly free itself from Man,
　Are calling to each other thro' a dawn
　Stranger than earth has ever seen ; the veil
　Is rending, and the Voices of the day
　Are heard across the Voices of the dark."

\* \* \*

"And we, the poor earth's dying race, and yet
　No phantoms, watching from a phantom shore
　Await the last and largest sense to make
　The phantom walls of this illusion fade,
　And show us that the world is wholly fair."

R. W. SIMPSON AND CO., LTD.,
PRINTERS,
RICHMOND AND LONDON.

# ARTHUR LOVELL'S WORKS.

*4th Edition.  Enlarged.*  **ARS VIVENDI.**    **2/-** *net*

*The Times.*—"This was published in 1896, the first of a series of Volumes expounding 'Ars Vivendism,'—that is, containing practical advice on the development of mind and body.  Five new chapters have now been added."

*The Literary World.*—"The Author suggests methods of strengthening the will, concentrating imagination, and stimulating a healthy, mental development on rational lines."

*The Pall Mall Gazette.*—"So sane and inspiriting an exposition of conservation of energy, and the acquirement of mental vigour as is to be found in the Author's earlier 'Ars Vivendi.'"

*The Bristol Mercury.*—"The book abounds in excellent advice, and the object is an admirable one."

*The Rock.*—"This marvellously sound and wholesome book.  In these pessimistic days it is a treat to meet so admirable a work so delightfully written."

## CONCENTRATION.

*2nd Edition, enlarged by a new chapter, 'Matter and Force,'* **2/-** *net.*

*The Spectator.*—"Mr. Lovell hints at a remedy for this state of things in concentration of mind in contrast to the dispersion of intellectual power which we see at work all around us."

Opinion of the Author of "*The Light of Asia*" :

"Sir Edwin Arnold returns grateful thanks to Mr. Lovell for the little book which he so kindly sent.  He has heard every word of it with profit and with pleasure, and has hardly any fault to find with it except that of its brevity."    OF  ALL  BOOKSELLERS.

**SIMPKIN, MARSHALL & Co., 4 Stationers' Hall Court, London, E.C.**

**GEO. ROBERTSON & Co., Prop., Ltd., Melbourne, Sydney, Adelaide & Brisbane.**

# DO  YOU  WANT  HEALTH WITHOUT  DRUGS ?

If so, read these books, which are recommended, and you will be able to cure yourself of any complaints on a scientific basis by mental means —not hypnotism if you rightly apply the directions given.

**BRAUN'S** "Mastery of Fate," 2 Vols. 2/6 each.

**WOOD'S** "Ideal Suggestion through Mental Photography," 2/6, cloth 5/6.

**WILMANS'** "Home Course in Mental Science," 20 lessons in separate covers, 21/-.

**HADDOCKS** "Power of Will," 9/-.

**INGALESE** "The History of Power and Mind," 8/6.

**EVANS'** "Divine Law of Cure," 6/6.

**DEWEY** ", The Way, Truth and Life," 8/6.

**BRADBURY'S** "Light in Thee," 3/6.

**BOEHME** "Seven Essays on Attainment of Happiness," 4/6.
  "Mental Healing made plain," 4/6.
  "Easy Lessons in Realization," 4/6.

**MULFORD'S** "White Cross Library," 6 Vols., 51/-, or 9/- single Vols.

If these books do not give satisfaction the cash will be returned, on receipt of Books in four days in good condition, providing this privilege is asked for when ordering

## AMERICAN BOOK AGENCY, DEVONPORT, DEVON.

All American Books stocked or procured by return mail.

CPSIA information can be obtained at www.ICGtesting.com
Printed in the USA
LVOW07s1807070116

469494LV00024B/1159/P